AUSTRALIA

Grace Jones

Image Credits

All images are courtesy of Shutterstock.com, unless otherwise specified. With thanks to Getty Images, Thinkstock Photo and iStockphoto.
Front Cover – rickyd, Tomas Kotouc, Christopher Robin Smith Photography. 1 – fritz16. 4&5 – metha1819. 6&7 – Rich Carey, Michael Potter11, AuntSpray, Andrea Danti. 8&9 – N Mrtgh, JackScott. 10&11 – By DiverDave (Own work) [CC BY-SA 3.0 (http://creativecommons. org/licenses/by-sa/3.0)], via Wikimedia Commons, Benny Marty, Eric Isselee, inavanhateren, Sanit Fuangnakhon, mark higgins, Valt Ahyppo, John Carnemolla, Tomas Kotouc, Alberto Loyo. 12&13 – Ng Toby, User:Peterdownunder, User:Diceman (Tasmania_location_ map.svg) [CC BY-SA 2.5-2.0-1.0 or CC BY-SA 2.5-2.0-1.0], via Wikimedia Commons, worldswildlifewonders. 14&15 – jeep2499, Peter J. Wilson, Manon van Os. 16&17 – Samantzis, idiz, Traveller Martin. 18&19 – Afterman, David Ongley, Drew McArthur. 20&21 – Puffin's Pictures, hubert, KarenHBlack. 22&23 – dirkr, wildestanimal, Rich Carey. 24&25 – EcoPrint, Julian W, Gapvoy, EpochCatcher. 26&27 – klauscook, vchal, EddieCloud, Lamberrto, wavebreakmedia, niall dunne.

BookLife
PUBLISHING

©2018
BookLife Publishing
King's Lynn
Norfolk PE30 4LS

ISBN: 978-1-78637-249-9

Written by:
Grace Jones

Edited by:
John Wood

Designed by:
Drue Rintoul

CONTENTS

Words that look like this are explained in the glossary on page 30.

ENDANGERED ANIMALS

Experts estimate that there are anywhere between two million and nine million **species** living on planet Earth today, but thousands of these are in danger of dying out every single year.

What Does It Mean If a Species Is Endangered?

Any species of plant or animal that is at risk of dying out completely is said to be endangered. When all individuals of a single species die, that species has become extinct.

Extinction is a real possibility for all species that are already threatened or endangered. Experts estimate that between 150 and 200 different species become extinct every day.

Dinosaurs are an example of an extinct species. They walked the Earth over 225 million years ago, and became extinct around 65 million years ago.

The International Union for Conservation of Nature and Natural Resources (IUCN) is the main **organisation** that records which species are in danger of extinction. The species are put into different categories, from the most to the least threatened with extinction.

IUCN'S CATEGORIES OF THREATENED ANIMALS

Category	Explanation
Extinct	Species that have no surviving members
Extinct in the Wild	Species with only surviving members in **captivity**
Critically Endangered	Species that have an extremely high risk of extinction in the wild
Endangered	Species that have a high risk of extinction in the wild
Vulnerable	Species that are likely to become endangered or critically endangered in the near future
Near Threatened	Species that are likely to become vulnerable or endangered in the near future
Least Concern	Species that fit into none of the above categories

The IUCN's work is extremely important. Once a species has been recognised as 'at risk', organisations and **governments** will often take steps to protect the species and its **habitats** in order to save it from extinction. The practice of protecting or conserving a species and its habitats is called **conservation**.

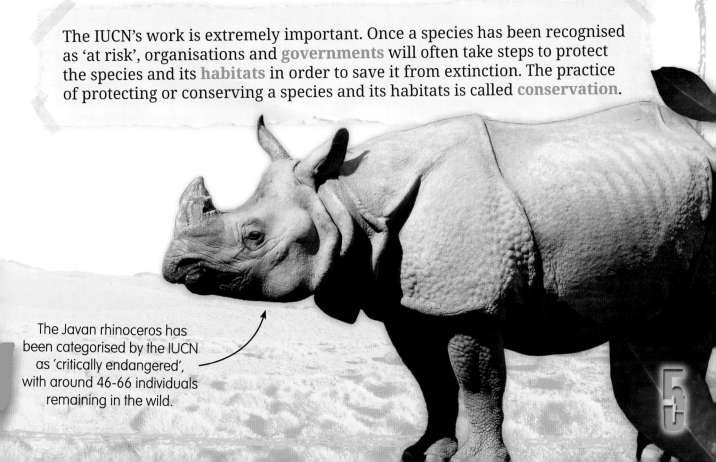

The Javan rhinoceros has been categorised by the IUCN as 'critically endangered', with around 46-66 individuals remaining in the wild.

WHY DO ANIMALS BECOME ENDANGERED?

Over the last 100 years, the human population of the world has grown by over 4.5 billion people. As the population has grown, the damage humans do to the environment and wildlife has increased too. Many experts believe that human activity is the biggest threat to animals around the world today.

Habitat Destruction

One of the biggest threats species face is the loss of their habitats. Large areas of land are often used to build settlements to provide more housing, food and natural resources for the growing world population. This can often destroy natural habitats, which nearby wildlife need in order to survive.

POLLUTION

Pollution is the introduction of harmful waste to the air, water or land. Pollution threatens wildlife all over the world; for example, people drop litter, which can cut, choke or even poison animals.

To use land for housing or farming, all the trees must be cut down and cleared from the area. This is called deforestation.

HUNTERS AND POACHERS

Many species are endangered because of hunting or poaching. Throughout history, humans have hunted certain species of animal for their meat, fur, skin or tusks.

Male African elephants are hunted by poachers for their huge tusks, which are made from a natural material called ivory and are sold for lots of money.

The dodo was a species of bird that was hunted to extinction. The last time a dodo was seen alive was in 1662.

Natural Causes

While the most serious threats to animals are caused by humans, there are natural threats to animals too. For example, it is thought that the extinction of the dinosaurs was caused by a natural event, when a meteorite hit the Earth. Other species may become extinct because they are not as well adapted to survive in their environments as others. Experts believe that the number of species that become extinct due to human activity is around 1,000 times more than those becoming extinct through natural causes.

AUSTRALIA

Australia is one of the seven continents of the world. Continents are large areas of land that, along with five oceans, make up the Earth's surface. The other six continents are: Africa, Antarctica, Asia, Europe, North America and South America. Australia is the smallest continent in the world. There are three oceans that surround Australia. The Pacific Ocean lies on the east coast of Australia, the Indian Ocean to the west and the Southern Ocean, which is sometimes called the Antarctic Ocean, to the south.

CONTINENTS OF THE WORLD

DO YOU KNOW WHICH CONTINENT YOU LIVE IN?

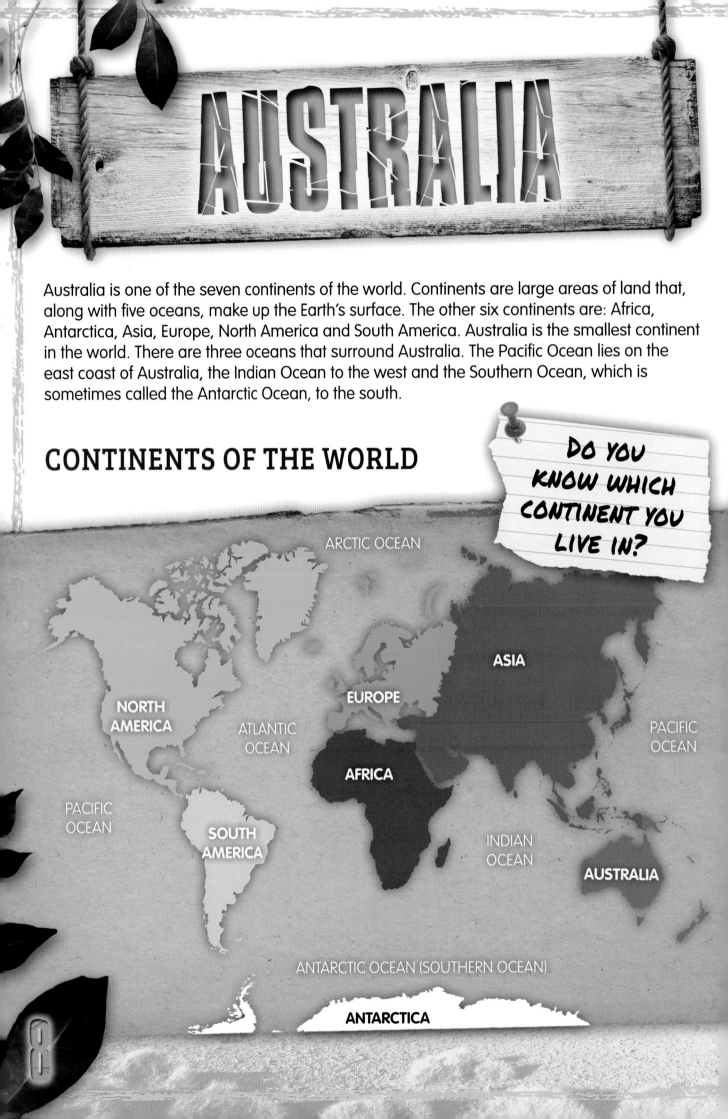

ARCTIC OCEAN

ASIA

EUROPE

NORTH AMERICA

ATLANTIC OCEAN

PACIFIC OCEAN

AFRICA

PACIFIC OCEAN

SOUTH AMERICA

INDIAN OCEAN

AUSTRALIA

ANTARCTIC OCEAN (SOUTHERN OCEAN)

ANTARCTICA

FACTS ABOUT AUSTRALIA

FACTFILE

Population: Over 24 million people.

Land Area: Over 7.6 million square kilometres (km).

Highest Peak: Mount Kosciuszko in New South Wales, Australia, rises to 2,228 metres (m) above sea level.

Longest River: The River Murray is the longest river in Australia and it is approximately 2,520 km long.

Biggest Country by Area: Australia, which is over 7.69 million square km.

Main Language Spoken: English.

Mount Kosciuszko

Wildlife and Habitats

There are many different types of habitat found across the Australian continent, including scrublands, woodlands, deserts and marine habitats. One of the most famous habitats is the Great Barrier Reef, which is a coral reef that stretches for around 2,300 km along Australia's north-eastern coastline. It is home to over 1,500 species of fish.

AROUND 35% OF AUSTRALIA'S LAND IS FLAT, DRY DESERT, WHICH GETS VERY LITTLE RAINFALL THROUGHOUT THE YEAR.

Great Victoria Desert

9

ENDANGERED AUSTRALIAN ANIMALS

One of the biggest threats facing Australia's wildlife today is habitat destruction. In particular, deforestation is threatening many habitats and species across Australia. Also, **commercial fishing** around Australia's coastlines is damaging the marine habitats and species that live along them. According to the IUCN, there are over 86 species of animal that are critically endangered in Australia today.

10 ANIMALS IN DANGER IN AUSTRALIA

1

Tasmanian Devil

Conservation Status:
Endangered

Number:
Unknown – in 2007, the number was thought to be between 25,000–10,000

2

Koala

Conservation Status:
Vulnerable

Number:
Between 100,000–500,000 adults in the wild

3

Great Desert Skink

Conservation Status:
Vulnerable

Number:
Over 5,000

4

Southern Cassowary

Conservation Status:
Vulnerable

Number:
6,000–15,000 adults living in the wild

5

Northern Hairy-Nosed Wombat

Conservation Status:
Critically Endangered

Number:
Around 115

6

Green and Golden Bell Frog

Conservation Status:
Vulnerable

Number:
Unknown

7

Northern Quoll

Conservation Status:
Endangered

Number:
Unknown

8

Australian Sea Lion

Conservation Status:
Endangered

Number:
Around 6,500

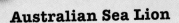

9

Grey-Headed Flying Fox

Conservation Status:
Vulnerable

Number:
Around 674,000

10

Bridled Nailtail Wallaby

Conservation Status:
Vulnerable

Number:
Between 800–1,100

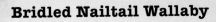

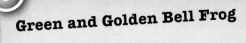

11

TASMANIAN DEVIL

FACTFILE

**Number Living
in the Wild:** Unknown – in 2007 the number was
thought to be between 25,000–10,000

IUCN Status: Endangered

Scientific Name: *Sarcophilus harrisii*

Weight: Between 4-12 kilograms (kg)

Size: Between 50-77 centimetres (cm) long

Life Span: Up to 5 years

Habitat: Coastal scrublands and forests

Diet: Carnivore

Tasmanian Devil

Where Do They Live?

The Tasmanian devil is only
found on the island of Tasmania.
The species disappeared from
the Australian mainland around
430 years ago. Although they
prefer coastal scrublands and
forests, the Tasmanian devil
lives all over the island.

Key

Oceans
and Seas

Land

Tasmanian Devil
Habitats

Pacific
Ocean

AUSTRALIA

Indian
Ocean

TASMANIA

WHY ARE THEY IN DANGER?

Tasmanian devil populations have declined by 90% in the last ten years because of an incurable disease called devil facial tumour disease (DFTD). DFTD causes large lumps to grow around the Tasmanian devil's head and mouth, which makes it very difficult for the animal to eat. Eventually, the lumps become so large that the animal is unable to eat at all and it starves to death.

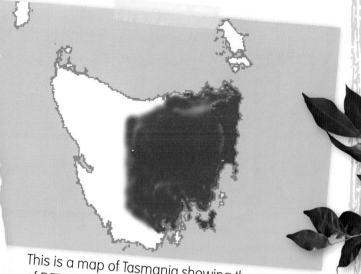

This is a map of Tasmania showing the spread of DFTD in Tasmanian devil populations in 2008.

DFTD HASN'T SPREAD TO ALL OF THE WILD POPULATIONS OF TASMANIAN DEVILS LIVING IN TASMANIA, BUT IT CAN SPREAD VERY QUICKLY AND WILL ALMOST CERTAINLY END IN DEATH.

How Are They Being Protected?

The Save the Tasmanian Devil Program began in 2003 with the aim of saving the species from extinction. Over the years, they have increased the amount of captive breeding programmes in order to release healthy Tasmanian devils back into the wild. There have also been efforts to find diseased Tasmanian devils in wild populations and remove them from the area so they do not pass the disease onto others. The programme has been given more funding to research possible cures and treatments for the deadly disease. However, a cure can take a very long time and one may never be found.

KOALA

FACTFILE

Number Living in the Wild: Between 100,000–500,000 living in the wild

IUCN Status: Vulnerable

Scientific Name: *Phascolarctos cinereus*

Weight: Adults can weigh between 4–15 kg

Size: 60–85 cm long

Life Span: Between 13–18 years in the wild

Habitat: Eucalyptus trees

Diet: Herbivore

Koala

Where Do They Live?

Koalas live in woodland and forest areas that have lots of eucalyptus trees, which are their main food source.

Key

Oceans and Seas

Land

Koala Habitats

Pacific Ocean

AUSTRALIA

Indian Ocean

Why Are They in Danger?

During the late 19th and early 20th centuries, millions of koalas were killed for their skins and furs. This practice was made **illegal** in the 20th century, but the koala population has never recovered. Since then, koalas have faced threats from habitat destruction, disease and natural disasters, such as **bushfires** and **droughts**.

HOW ARE THEY BEING PROTECTED?

In much of the koala's range, there are conservation and recovery plans in place to protect them and their habitats. There are also many captive breeding programmes in place throughout the world to ensure koala populations remain stable in the future. Many of the koalas that are bred in captivity are reintroduced back into the wild too. However, much more needs to be done to protect koala habitats to help numbers increase in the future.

NORTHERN HAIRY-NOSED WOMBAT

FACTFILE

Number Living in the Wild: Around 115

IUCN Status: Critically Endangered

Scientific Name: *Lasiorhinus krefftii*

Weight: Up to 40 kg

Size: Up to 1 m long

Life Span: Up to 6 years in the wild

Habitat: Sandy, grassy woodland

Diet: Herbivore

Northern Hairy-Nosed Wombat

Where Do They Live?

Northern hairy-nosed wombats live in sandy, grassy woodland in two places in the north-east of Australia. These two places are called Epping Forest National Park and Richard Underwood Nature Refuge.

Key

Oceans and Seas

Land

Northern Hairy-Nosed Wombat Habitats

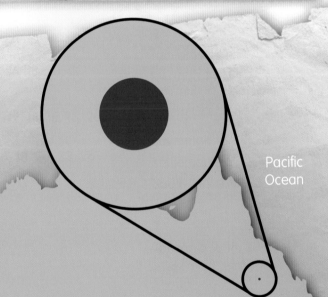

Pacific Ocean

AUSTRALIA

Indian Ocean

WHY ARE THEY IN DANGER?

Because the population of the northern hairy-nosed wombat is so low, the species is most at risk from natural events, such as floods and droughts. For example, a six-year drought in the 1990s damaged the health of the wombat population very badly. In turn, they had fewer babies, and the overall population became smaller. Habitat destruction has also affected the population, which is why northern hairy-nosed wombats can now only be found in the wild in two very small areas of Queensland.

How Are They Being Protected?

Food and water stations have been put in place in Epping Forest National Park to provide the northern hairy-nosed wombat with food and water in times of need, such as during a drought. To make sure that the species does not become extinct in the future, the Australian **government** have funded research into finding new habitats that are suitable for the northern hairy-nosed wombat to live in. **Conservationists** hope that one day they can release captive members of the species into these new habitats in the hope of saving the species from future extinction.

SOUTHERN CASSOWARY

FACTFILE

Number Living in the Wild: 6,000–15,000 adults

IUCN Status: Vulnerable

Scientific Name: *Casuarius casuarius*

Weight: Up to 60 kg

Size: Up to 2 m tall

Life Span: Unknown in the wild, but up to 60 years in captivity

Habitat: Rainforests and forests

Diet: Omnivore

Southern Cassowary

Where Do They Live?

Southern cassowaries live in rainforests and forests in small areas of northern Australia, Indonesia and Papua New Guinea.

Key

Oceans and Seas

Land

Southern Cassowary Habitats

Pacific Ocean

AUSTRALIA

Indian Ocean

Tropical Storm

Why Are They in Danger?

One of the biggest threats that southern cassowaries have faced has come from hunting. In Australia, Papua New Guinea and Indonesia they have been hunted in order to be eaten by people. Southern cassowaries are also being affected by natural disasters, such as tropical storms, which can destroy large parts of their habitats and food sources in a very small amount of time.

HOW ARE THEY BEING PROTECTED?

In 2002, a conservation plan began in Australia to protect southern cassowaries. This has included protecting and managing cassowary habitats. Temporary feeding stations have also been set up in those areas where food sources have been damaged by strong storms. However, the population of the species is still decreasing, which means that more conservation steps need to be taken to save southern cassowaries from extinction in the future.

GREY-HEADED FLYING FOX

FACTFILE

Number Living in the Wild: Around 674,000

IUCN Status: Vulnerable

Scientific Name: *Pteropus poliocephalus*

Weight: Between 600–1000 g

Size: Between 23–29 cm long

Life Span: Between 12–15 years in the wild

Habitat: Rainforests, woodlands, swamps and suburban areas

Diet: Herbivore

Grey-Headed Flying Fox

Where Do They Live?

Grey-headed flying foxes live in many different habitats including rainforests, woodlands, swamps and even suburban areas across eastern Australia.

Key

- Oceans and Seas
- Land
- Grey-Headed Flying Fox Habitats

Pacific Ocean

AUSTRALIA

Indian Ocean

WHY ARE THEY IN DANGER?

The biggest threat to grey-headed flying foxes is deforestation. This species feeds on fruit, nectar and pollen found on plants and trees. The destruction of forests to make room for farms, livestock and new buildings has left the species with fewer habitats where they can forage for their food. The lack of food sources has decreased the survival and reproduction rate of grey-headed flying foxes.

Figs

Grey-headed flying foxes often eat fruit such as figs. This is why they are sometimes called 'fruit bats'. They will often fly up to 50 km to forage for food.

How Are They Being Protected?

The Australian government has legally protected some of the grey-headed flying foxes' roosting sites. Roosting sites are places that the species uses to rest during the daytime. However, more conservation steps need to be taken to protect their habitats and food sources. Further steps are being taken to make sure that more grey-headed flying foxes are bred in captivity too. Breeding in captivity has been very successful so far and could be one way to help protect this species from extinction in the future.

AUSTRALIAN SEA LION

FACTFILE

Number Living in the Wild: Around 6,500

IUCN Status: Endangered

Scientific Name: *Neophoca cinerea*

Weight: Females can weigh up to 105 kg and males 300 kg

Size: Females are between 1.5–1.7 m long and males 1.8–2.5 m long

Life Span: Between 12–16 years in the wild

Habitat: Marine habitats in and around the southern and south-western coastlines of Australia

Diet: Carnivore

Australian Sea Lion

Where Do They Live?

Australian sea lions live in large groups, called colonies, in marine habitats in and around the southern and south-western coastlines of Australia.

Key

Oceans and Seas

Land

Australian Sea Lion Habitats

Pacific Ocean

AUSTRALIA

Indian Ocean

Gillnet

Why Are They in Danger?

The population of Australian sea lions has declined a lot in the last century because they have been heavily hunted for their furs. Although hunting has now been made illegal, the species still faces threats from commercial fishing. Australian sea lions are becoming tangled and caught in commercial fishing nets. Sea lions must come to the surface of the water to breathe, meaning they will die if they become caught in fishing nets.

THE AUSTRALIAN SEA LION POPULATION IS NOW SO SMALL THAT IT IS THE RAREST SEA LION SPECIES IN THE WORLD.

HOW ARE THEY BEING PROTECTED?

In 2010, the Australian Fisheries Management Authorities (AFMA) introduced a range of measures to change the gill nets that the Australian sea lions are most often trapped in. Conservationists hope that this action will prevent the death of thousands of sea lions in the future.

AUSTRALIAN SEA LIONS HAVE VERY SENSITIVE WHISKERS WHICH ALLOW THEM TO DETECT MOVEMENT IN DARK WATERS IN ORDER TO FIND A MEAL.

AUSTRALIA IN THE FUTURE

Many steps have already been taken to protect wildlife and conserve habitats throughout Australia, but much more can still be done to save endangered animals from extinction.

Protecting Habitats

Australia's habitats are some of the most well-protected in the world. The National Reserve System (NRS) is a network of legally protected land areas that are mostly owned by the Australian government. By protecting these areas, the government hopes to conserve the environment and its wildlife for years to come. Over 17% of Australia's land is protected by the NRS, which includes around 137 million hectares of land and over 10,000 protected sites.

Kakadu National Park, Australia

Numbat

With few areas left that endangered species can call home, immediate action must be taken if they are to be saved from extinction in the future.

24

EDUCATION

Education is one of the most important tools we have when helping animals in danger. Education about the wildlife around us and the important part it plays within our world can often be enough to change negative attitudes. It is not only important to educate children, adults and communities, but also the industries that threaten endangered animals. For example, recent conservation efforts to protect Australia's marine species have included educating people who work within the fishing industry on the damage commercial fishing can do to animals in the sea.

Education within the fishing industry is helping to protect endangered Australian species like the Australian sea lion.

Wildlife Tourism

Many wildlife organisations, charities and governments around the world are using the money that is made from wildlife tourism to protect endangered animals throughout Australia. The Australia Zoo in Queensland receives over 700,000 visitors a year. Much of the money that the zoo makes from wildlife tourism is used to fund conservation projects throughout Australia and the rest of the world. For example, Australia Zoo helps to fund the Save the Tasmanian Devil Program in order to help find a cure to DFTD and to protect the remaining wild population.

HOW CAN I MAKE A DIFFERENCE?

1 CAMPAIGN WITH AN ORGANISATION

Wildlife organisations such as WWF and Greenpeace have helped to save many endangered species and even convince countries to change the laws through campaigning.

2 DONATE TO A CHARITY YOU BELIEVE IN

You can usually donate as little or as much as you want and most charities show you how your donations are helping to make a difference.

3 LEARN MORE ABOUT ENDANGERED SPECIES IN YOUR AREA

One of the most important ways to protect endangered species is by understanding the threats that they face. Visit a local wildlife refuge, national park or reserve or join a local wildlife organisation.

4 ADOPT AN ANIMAL

Your donation will normally go to feeding and looking after the animal that you have adopted. You'll usually get an adoption certificate and regular updates on how your animal is doing.

5 HELP TO RAISE AWARENESS BY TALKING TO OTHERS

It is important that we all talk about issues that may threaten wildlife throughout the world. By talking about these issues, it can help to make people aware of how they may be affecting wildlife and encourage them to take steps to prevent harm.

6 VOLUNTEER AT A LOCAL WILDLIFE CHARITY OR SHELTER

It is not only endangered animals who are in danger; we should help to care for all of the animals in the world.

FIND OUT MORE

To find out more about endangered species in Australia and what you can do to get involved with conservation efforts, visit:

Australia Zoo
www.australiazoo.com.au/conservation/

Australian Wildlife Conservancy (AWF)
www.australianwildlife.org/

International Union for Conservation of Nature (IUCN)
www.iucnredlist.org

World Wide Fund for Nature (WWF)
www.worldwildlife.org

To discover more about other endangered animals around the world take a look at more books in this series:

Asia, Endangered Animals
Grace Jones (BookLife, 2018)

North America, Endangered Animals
Grace Jones (BookLife, 2018)

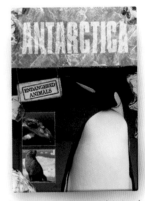
Antarctica, Endangered Animals
Grace Jones (BookLife, 2018)

Africa, Endangered Animals
Grace Jones (BookLife, 2018)

Europe, Endangered Animals
Grace Jones (BookLife, 2018)

South America, Endangered Animals
Grace Jones (BookLife, 2018)

QUICK QUIZ

1. HOW MANY NORTHERN HAIRY-NOSED WOMBATS ARE LIVING IN THE WILD?

2. WHAT IS THE SCIENTIFIC NAME OF THE SOUTHERN CASSOWARY?

3. WHAT DO GREY-HEADED FLYING FOXES EAT?

4. HOW MUCH DO KOALAS WEIGH?

5. HOW LONG DO AUSTRALIAN SEA LIONS USUALLY LIVE FOR?

6. WHAT IS THE IUCN CONSERVATION STATUS OF THE TASMANIAN DEVIL?

For answers see the bottom of page 32.

GLOSSARY

adapted	changed over time to suit different conditions
bushfires	fires in scrublands or forests that usually spread quickly
captive breeding programmes	programmes focused on producing young from animals that are cared for by humans
captivity	when animals are cared for by humans and not living in the wild
carnivore	animals that eat other animals rather than plants
commercial fishing	fishing companies who make money from large-scale fishing
conservation	the practice of protecting or conserving a species and its habitats
conservationists	people who act for the protection of wildlife and the environment
deforestation	the action of cutting down trees on large areas of land
droughts	long periods of very little rainfall, which leads to a lack of water
environment	the natural world
forage	search for food

governments	groups of people with the authority to run a country and decide its laws
habitats	the natural environments in which animals or plants live
herbivore	an animal that only eats plants
illegal	forbidden by law
incurable	cannot be cured or treated
livestock	animals that are kept for farming purposes
marine	relating to the sea
meteorite	a piece of rock that successfully enters a planet's atmosphere without being destroyed
natural resources	useful materials that are created by nature
omnivore	an animals that eats both other animals and plants
organisation	a group of people that work together to achieve the same goals
poaching	the act of the illegal capturing or killing of wild animals
population	the number of people living in a place
reproduction rate	the speed at which animals produce young
scrubland	land with shrubs or small trees on it
settlements	places people live permanently, like villages or towns
species	a group of very similar animals or plants that are capable of producing young together
suburban	areas just outside of a town or city
wildlife tourism	the actions and industry behind attracting people to visit new places to see wildlife

1. Around 115 **2.** Casuarius casuarius **3.** Fruit, nectar and pollen
4. 4–15 kilograms **5.** Between 12–16 years in the wild **6.** Endangered